Love Thy Self

By Debra A. Antney

Acknowledgements:

First and foremost, I want to thank God

Raleek and Red, I did it!

I thank my mother Millie Antney, who birthed me. I love you.

To all my siblings, blood and not blood, I love you guys to life.

And my 5 heartbeats, including my 2 angel sons, Monique and Veronica, I love you with all my heart.

Sherry, guess what? We shut Dre Carter's mouth...

I also want to thank Omara Harris

and Tina Brinkley Potts

for having my back.

There are so many people that helped me on my journey, good and bad. Every lesson was valuable. I thank you. Sorry it too me so long to grow up.

Copyright © 2023 by Debra A. Antney

All rights reserved. No part of this book may be used or reproduced by any means, graphic, electronic, or mechanical, including photocopying, recording, taping, or by any information storage retrieval system, without the written permission of the publisher except in the case of brief quotations embodied in critical articles and reviews.

Contents

We're All Average 4

What Is Love? 10

I've Earned It 14

P.U.S.S.Y. Is Power 16

Settling For What? 22

Why Hate On Me? 27

Watch That Mouth! 32

Voluntary Surrender 37

More "Likes Than Love 42

Thirsty By Nature?? 45

Are You Down With O.P.P.? If Not, You Better Get Down With It! 51

Whose Is It? 53

Stress 63

Self Preservation 72

When I'm out and about in cities across America, especially where I call home (within the metropolitan Atlanta area), I am constantly meeting women who ask for my advice on issues ranging from the mundane to the intimately personal. I do not mind these women asking me things, nor do I consider them an unwanted intrusion. Even when they bring up the weirdest shit, I listen earnestly and, if possible, give what advice I can. It is an experienced woman's obligation to share her acquired knowledge with other women. We of the female gender should always help one another when and if we can.

Way back when, I used to wonder why Not just women but people, period, came to me with their problems? It was as if I were a lightning rod waiting to be struck by someone else's drama. I was clueless for a while. Then, as time ticked and the world turned, the answer hit me like a bolt from the blue.

Being placed in a high (or fortunate) position, like a lightning rod, is my purpose. I'm meant to prevent damage by intervening between people and their problems. As the eldest of nine, I did a great deal of verbal and hands-on counseling with my siblings growing up. I've always been a manager of sorts.

Advocating and organizing the lives of others has been my job since adolescence. If I wasn't good at it, I never would have switched careers in my thirties and turned a sagacious nature along with a gift for gab into a thriving company that has represented several multiplatinum hip hop artists while earning a comfortable living in the process.

This is why I have created the MINI-M.E.G. series. This series comprises several well-thought-out guides capable of uplifting and centering any woman while assisting her in ascertaining her purpose, uplifting her spirit, and giving her the necessary tools to build a life instead of being content with existing. This first guide is "LOVE THY SELF." It is essential for every woman to learn to do so to thrive as nature intended for us to.

These are guides. These guides are not capable of making the journey for any woman. That's something only you, THE READER, are capable of. To receive motivation and be empowered, one must accept the process. For instance, you can only buy a new car on credit if you have established said credit. This is what Loving Self does. It creates a solid foundation of self-love, which can be built upon to each woman's specifications. You cannot have the life you desire when you cannot love your SELF. A woman loving her SELF is the first step in the process. The initial rung of the ladder to the top begins with a woman's first uplifting step towards the love of SELF.

WE'RE ALL AVERAGE

(Until We're Not)

By societal standards, I was average. In some ways, I'm still an average chick with exceptional wit who has been fortunate enough to survive, examine life, and grow from my own shit. There will always be those who attach some specialness to my name because of my celebrity, but I've always been exceptional. Understand that my specialness created my celebrity and not the other way around. All of us women are average {until we're not}. This means when we {women} choose to exercise our individual potential, we appear extraordinarily unique to others when we just opt to exemplify our true nature.

I ask those reading this guide -

Debra A. Antney

"WHO AMONG US WILL SHED THEIR AVERAGE SHELL TO SHARE HER EXTRAORDINARY GIFTS WITH THE WORLD?"

The caterpillar isn't much to look at. It's considered average, while the butterfly is celebrated for its unique and transcendent beauty. Think about this . . . The first crawls carefully everywhere, hoping fervently not to be stepped on or preyed upon. The other flies around joyfully in a spectacular array of showmanship being admired. Are you ready for this? They are one and the same! {sarcasm added}

Examine the caterpillar's daily hardships and even harsher conditions, constantly under threat of being crushed. Most who witness the caterpillar's journey view it as unattractive and do not appreciate its struggle. Isn't this the plight of most women in the world? We are judged by the opinions of others and unappreciated for our struggles. How often has a successful or seemingly beautiful woman admitted to being abused or feeling inadequate? Then, they, just like the caterpillar, tell us of their magical transformation.

Love Thy Self

This miraculous metamorphosis of the crawling caterpillar into the joyful butterfly is indicative of a woman's life who chooses to love SELF.

When women dare to be different, we are destined to be better. Those of us who neglect to love SELF completely continue to endure the pain and pressures of existence, deluding ourselves into believing it is just our lot in life to suffer. These women have lost their fucking minds and lack common sense. I get it! While I've always had common sense, I have not always exercised it. Oh yes! I have done plenty of Debbie dumb shit, but thankfully I've learned to use commonsense.

When?

Consistently.

How?

With care for my well-being.

What about us who won't use the good sense God gave them? It's okay that you stepped in some shit if you are willing to clean it up and learn from the experience. Dealing with some shit occasionally is good for the soul and future road a woman is journeying on. It keeps us sharp. The old axiom of a soldier never knowing their true strength without a foe comes to mind. We need to be tested to find our flaws and weaknesses. You can't correct what you don't know is wrong.

Those of you who are pretending your shit doesn't stink, ain't real, it'll go away, or lazily waiting for someone else to deal with it while continuing to track it around stinking up your lives, I think two things about you;

1) You can't know any better.

2) You don't love yourself.

Love is not a dormant emotion. It requires "doing". Love will transform the average female into an extraordinary woman. Love of SELF will pick you up from seemingly crawling on the ground, afraid of being crushed, to flying high against the winds of adversity, reaching the heights of success you were always destined for.

I used to put my panties on one leg at a time before realizing how much time, effort, and money I'd save by not wearing any. I'm making light of things, but a woman needs to prioritize or be held captive to the whim or running to the whistle of others. Love thy SELF is priority number one. From my mature experience, we women are the world's best pretenders. We pretend to love ourselves while showing love to everyone else. Husband, boyfriend, girlfriend, wife, children, family, friends, and neighbors alike. Fuck! Even pets receive the love and attention that we refuse to show SELF.

This guide, LOVE THY SELF, is based on a former project of mine titled THE LOVE YOURSELF LETTERS. Using social media and BE100 internet radio each week for several months, I wrote a letter to the global masses of women to engender self-love. When a woman loves herself, no amount of hate or lack of the appearance of love coming from external sources can impede her upward progress on the ladder of living a successful life.

The following topics serve as motivators, empowering you to find a more significant, unconditional love of SELF. Please allow me to be your guide, but don't hold me responsible if the answers you seek aren't found. Search harder and be accountable in pursuing what you're looking for.

WHAT IS LOVE?

Although love has one true definition, it means different things to different people. What does it mean to you? Answering that takes a few minutes, hours, days, and/or weeks. It may take some of you a few minutes and others a few months or even years to answer. Until you find this out, you will be incapable of completely loving your SELF. Love requires perpetual momentum. It moves like the wind. You may not see it; depending on your mood, you might not even feel it, but it's always present.

If LOVE were a person, it would be more potent than any man or more compassionate than any woman. It would be self-sacrificing and loyal beyond imagination, incapable of deceit and always having your back better than your spine. It would be the most beautiful, giving person in the entire universe. I don't know about you, but I want to fuck with LOVE. I want to sleep with it, wake up to it. Speak with it in a language that only we both intimately understand. I want LOVE to caress my soul while covering my body. I want to yell and tell the world:

"MOTHERFUCKERS LYING!! REAL LOVE DOESN'T HURT! IT FEELS GREAT!!"

LOVE is eternal joy, which need not explain its presence in your life, because its actions speak volumes. A few things will tell you when you have this kind of love for SELF.

- a) You won't hate on yourself & will thank those who do
- b) You feel good about who you are
- c) You are not only giving to SELF, but others as well

Remember, LOVE has one definition but means different things to different people, but here's what you, dear reader, need to know . . . LOVE IS THE DEFINITIVE DEFINITION OF LIFE. So, if you are not

Love Thy Self

loving yourself, you aren't living. And we all know that if you aren't alive, you are D-E-A-D, dead. The dead don't live life; they can't help the living, and life is of no concern. But when a woman has a love for SELF, she is more alive than a newborn. The possibilities of each day are infinite, and although she may not know what she wants, she knows that she can get it when she finds out.

Throughout humankind, men and women have deceived each other into accepting and adopting their own self-serving definition of love instead of edifying one's self on how to love SELF. By learning to love SELF, you'll become educated on how to love others and accept real love when it introduces itself into your life. There will be no acts of self-sabotage or willfully chasing lust disguised as love. For those who are slow to comprehend, that means being overcome by the dis-ease of GOOD DICK or W.et A.ss P. ussy, depending on your sexual preference. BEWARE OF GOOD DICK and WAP! Yes, there is such a thing. Great sex has knocked out some of the female gender's greatest assets.

Debra A. Antney

This leads us to address the hot topic of P.U.S.S.Y. IS POWER. Some of us give our power away, and some have it taken from us..

I'VE EARNED IT

THEY claim Pussy is powerful
never been one, so I don't know
Knowledge, persistence, and true aim
is what keeps me running my show.

SOME say good Dick to Pussy
is like knockout kryptonite.
From skinny teen to mature thickness-
ask any Dick, I've never lost a fight

A FEW claiming while they shaming
"Power is in the Pussy
if it has a tight grip".
I bet Pussy ain't never thought this,
let alone ran its lips.

I earned mine!

Debra A. Antney

THEY stupid!
Some need to get they shit together,
sadly FEW ever do.
Real power is how a woman thinks
not what her Pussy do - DEBRA ANTNEY

P.U.S.S.Y. IS POWER

{Legs Open/Pocketbooks Closed}

Patently Understanding Sex Sells You is POWER in the world where we women live. The statement comes with this clarifier; A woman's actual physical vagina/pussy, has no true power outside of producing life and bringing pleasure. It is the idea and/or imagination of our pussies that have and hold real power. Once we give in to the reality of our pussies, we lose our power. Now, for those of us who are slow, this means that whoever desires your sex will continue to desire it if their imagination or ideas concerning your sex aren't disrupted by reality.

In their mind, your pussy is tighter than the grip of a hungry boa constrictor. Smells like fresh-cut flowers on a spring day and tastes like peaches & cream. It is wetter than the shoreline of a tropical beach and hotter than the sun that shines down on it. Its lips are softer and more supple than a newly formed cloud, and it is the only place they want to forever be. That is their ideas and imaginative thoughts. Here's the reality: After multiple children, that same pussy could use Kegel exercises. It no longer smells like fresh-cut flowers at the end of a good day's work. It smells like the fish in the waters off that tropical shoreline and tastes nothing close to fruit but more like stale water.

Once the reality sets in, the magic and the mystique are gone. They no longer want your pussy because your pussy doesn't coincide with their imagination and idea of what pussy should be like. Keep in mind that on real women, our pussies aren't detachable, so this means if they don't want the pussy, they don't want the rest of the package the pussy came with. What if we kept our LEGS CLOSED and our POCKETBOOKS OPEN? Meaning what if we focused on taking care of ourselves instead of pleasuring them? Not just from a monetary

Love Thy Self

perspective but from a °360-degree perspective. MIND/BODY/SOUL!

Patently understanding sex sells you is about understanding that pussy is a product, but the thought of pussy is a high commodity. What's the difference, Ms. Deb? Well, a product is sold at market and used. At the same time, a commodity is something useful that can be turned into commercial or other advantage, also traded on the global stock markets. To give the Reader an analogy: Some of the women who are reading this have used their pussies like an easy pass at a subway turnstile to get from destination to destination, constantly standing on what looks like the same platform. While others reading this have treated their pussies like a high commodity, trading the thought of it to advance or acquire something advantageous for themselves.

LEGS CLOSED/POCKETBOOKS OPEN isn't about sack chasing or gold-digging. Keeping your legs closed is about a woman not selling herself short by fucking everything that comes her way. Instead, she opens up her pocketbook/bag, which is a metaphor for her (MIND), and uses the skills at her disposal (i.e., the things in her mind) to increase her successes and style of life without compromising her reputation or the values & morals she's founded upon.

Look inside your pocketbook, purse, bag, or whatever you're carrying right now, and lay all the items on a flat surface. Check this out: most women can care for a small group of people with the items in their pocketbooks. There might be a change of clothes or children's clothes. A good wig, hair extensions, tampons, food & drink, money, medication, household tools, et cetera. All the things that you need to take care of your business. Shouldn't the pocketbook of your mind be the same way? Shouldn't you have plenty of mental tools ready to be used for your benefit?

Some women are preening like peacocks, bragging to anyone who'll listen about how great intercourse is with their partner(s). Cool Beans, but the women I find super irritating are going crazy over that "good dick." It's okay to give credit where credit is due, but damn, don't go ga ga goofy over an orgasm you can give yourself. Is the "good dick" attached to an even better MAN? Does the attention he pays you in bed pale compared to the attention he pays you out of bed?

In the same way sex sells a woman, it can bankrupt her, also. Yes, sometimes financially, but I'm speaking more about emotional bankruptcy. Some of us get so wrapped up in a man's phallus that we mistakenly associate his erect penis as an instrument of power in our lives, allowing ourselves to have our identity taken away and replaced with whatever identity is given to us. This is how we end up playing positions of BITCH, HOE, BABY MOMA, and SIDE CHICK instead of holding down positions such as CEO, CHILDREN'S MOTHER, and BOSS CHICK. Every penis needs a plug; for the most part, we're IT!

We are the "plug" or connection that must be made if a heterosexual man wants to fulfill his sexual desires. This connection is far more profound than our vaginal sheath. I'm referring to a mental, spiritual, and financial connection. Why not withhold your sexual favors until you find out if you and this man are compatible? P.U.S.S.Y. IS POWER! Understanding that your sex is a significant selling point in your relationships gives you the power to analyze your demographic and market yourself accordingly for optimum return.

This means you are not needlessly exposing yourself to disease, disappointment, or the stress of dysfunctional relationships because you are aware of the power of P.U.S.S.Y! You don't move on the basis that your sex is drooling like the village idiot throbbing for coital contact. You are the woman who moves off of the basis of what is good for her right now and in the near future. YOU are the woman that refuses to bow to a dick or SETTLE.

SETTLING FOR WHAT?

Most of us have already settled or become comfortable with accepting our position, and some of us endure resignedly. Some of you think to endure or accept your fate must be done to continue to exist. Settling requires any woman, regardless of age, race, religion, or sexual orientation, to do nothing and participate passively in their own life. Usually, those who simply exist believe there are no options other than those given or presented by external sources. These "external" sources really could care less about your growth and well-being as long as you're doing what they need you to do.

Life often comes down to what we will or won't accept, along with our choices. More importantly, how we see ourselves. We all have encountered and known that brutal bitch, REFLECTION. She doesn't alter what stands before her, but the woman looking at herself can and very often does.

Debra A. Antney

When we don't love ourselves, it shows in two ways: The behavior we allow and the behavior we exhibit. Both can lead to us settling.

Self-hatred or indifference of self can easily cause us to take whatever is offered, even if that offering is beneath our value level. When neglecting to love ourselves, the image we see in the mirror is a fallacy created by our self-loathing. We can't trust the image in the mirror because we can't trust the woman viewing the image being presented. This is the grand deception of self.

All women are beautiful in our own respects, but we don't often focus on self beauty. Instead, we dwell on what others deem negative about us. Why? Why aren't we focusing on those positive attributes that we know we have. Why aren't we cultivating and accentuating the beauty we see in ourselves? Usually, because we have been taught to settle for someone else's image of us. Settle? Heaven's forbid. I learned long ago that settling was not my thing. In order to accept whatever image someone else had for me, I would've needed

Love Thy Self

to purposely neglect my skills and natural talents. At one point, I couldn't do better because I didn't know any better. If you knew better, wouldn't you do better?

I'd like to share a very personal story with you . . . . It was a long time ago. I was young with perky tits, tight hips, and thinking no one could smell my shit. Let me tell it, nothing exited this ass except roses and Spring Fresh Febreeze. I think I was twenty or twenty-one in a relationship with a man fifteen years my senior. Need I say, I thought "Good Dick" was not only a cure-all but an amusement ride that admitted only me. Talk about wrong! I was convinced he loved me and had my best interest at heart. If you don't know the type, listen to Jazmine Sullivan's Heaux Tales album, specifically the song, Put It Down. In hindsight, my feelings weren't based on common sense or rational thought. Offer me a million bucks to tell you five things I actually loved about this Good Dick having man and my bank balance would not budge one cent.

Debra A. Antney

We think because we are joined at our pubic mounds, it amounts to something when it actually doesn't amount to a hill of beans. Sometimes, sex is just sex, and what we believe is love is really good sex! Without any reciprocity being shown, we take it upon ourselves to settle and label our relationship with our significant other as love when it is only sexual relations. I chose the above example because relationships are usually the starting point for a woman to settle in other areas of her life.

Now, back to this man who was fifteen years my senior. We shared an apartment together. He paid the bills, gave me money, and fucked my brains out, leaving me with little commonsense and nothing else that actually belonged to me. I found this out much later, after coming back to the apartment early and seeing my best friend sprawled across our bed like a playmate {in my nightie} while thinking it was my man coming to greet her. "No bitch, it's the real Debbie from the block!"

Love Thy Self

I whipped her, then fought with him (physically) as though we were headlining for UFC. Afterward, we argued like Republicans and Democrats until I grew tired of talking. The man had more game than an Evangelical preacher who was once a pimp with a penchant for articulate wordplay. I listened to every syllable, but it didn't mean shit! I was officially done as I gathered my things, preparing to leave.

My mother had come to the apartment to help me.

My advice is to never settle until you reach whatever your "TOP" is. Then when you get there, start looking for ways to find a helicopter, jet airplane, rocketship, or some motherfucking wings to fly to your next destination because, for a woman who won't settle, there is always another goal to accomplish or another place to be. SETTLING should never be an option for you, as it is never one for me!

WHY HATE ON ME?

Jealousy & Envy are twisted sisters with one shared agenda. They want to disrupt and bring negativity to your life. They operate in tandem or alone to ensure your life is unbalanced, essentially fucked up. Sometimes, these negative attributes work from within you. This means you're jealous or envious of others. However, Jealousy & Envy are mainly working against your person from those "EXTERNAL SOURCES" we addressed previously. They are two sides of the same coin. Not a quarter, dime, or even a plug nickel. The coin I'm referring to is one of hatred. In this generational era, to be jealous or green with envy, is to be a "HATER." What you should be asking is what I asked myself long ago: "WHY HATE ON ME?"

This is a question that every woman should be asking themselves. What makes us deserving of someone else's hatred? I went into deep contemplative meditation about this and came to

Love Thy Self

the conclusion that if I'm worth hating, then I'm undoubtedly worth loving. Maybe it's the love in me that draws haters like moths to a captive flame. It can't be the money or celebrity status. I'm practically sure of this because before the houses, cars, clothes, jewelry, and "Ms. Deb" came into play, Debbie Antney was hated. I was a broke chick with a lot of "Hollowers." Hating ass followers bent on seeing me fail.

Taking another meditative moment, I came up with this: If I was being hated way back when I was broke and still hated now, then it isn't about the material things that I have, insomuch as "who I am". I am no longer young, but I like to think I am always beautiful. Sure, thicker in the waist, still attractive in the face, the power of the P is tight, and I'm receiving no complaints from the opposite sex in the middle of the night. Cool beans! But something was still nagging me. What did I have then that I still have now? Stretch marks? Nah! Kids? Nah! Television shows? Nah! What in the hell did I have then that I still have today? ... Ambition?

Yep! Potential?Yep! A plan? Yep! A strong spirit, of course! But what I had then that I have even more now is I LOVE THY SELF.

Hollowers don't have a love for anyone and are exceedingly jealous of us women who practice self-love. They negatively envy those who apply the greatest, strongest emotion known to humankind. Isn't that something! Bitches are mad at us for loving us. Does that make sense? Some malicious, spiteful person is mad at me for loving me. Yeah, bitch please! And have you noticed that your hardest, hating follower usually tries pawning themselves off as your friend? Why the deception? Why come into our lives under the guise of friendship, trying to destroy our world with hatred?

Initially, I thought it was so they could hurt me, but leaving me alone (sarcastically saying) would do that. Would I be absolutely lost if my Hollowers were to vanish without a trace? Would you? What would we have to gauge ourselves against? What would we have to look at and tell ourselves, "Never be that miserable woman".

Instead of competing with myself, would I have to be competitive with other women who love themselves, or, would I become friends & associates with these like-minded spiritual feminine beings, using their intellect and self-love to exponentially increase my womanly worth? I continued contemplating, and it struck me the Hater is really just curious and wants to know the joys of self-love. Well damn! All a Hollower had to do was ask.

Any woman who chooses to exercise her God-given intelligence will realize that jealousy & envy are wasted emotions. Whoever has the time to practice hate against you is a loser; if you're doing it, so are you! It might sound harsh, though think about it. If you're focused on hating others, then you aren't concentrating on ways to build yourself or others up. This means you are not even in the game. You can never win and have already lost if you aren't in the game.

"Why hate on me?" is a question every woman should ask herself, but, "WHY AM I HATING ON MYSELF?" Is a problem that you should be solving as quickly as you can. START LOVING EVERYTHING ABOUT YOURSELF, EVEN IF YOU THINK IT'S BAD. Right now, I'm extending an olive branch to all those who are consistently jealous & envious of other people . . . THE HATER! Stop fighting a losing battle from a position of weakness. Stop smiling in the face of positive progress, waiting on real women to turn their backs so you can stick a knife in it. Stop standing on the sidelines, heckling and hating. Join the team and be a part of something great . . . WOMANHOOD.

Stop hating on yourself, and you'll never be accused of hating on someone else because there'll be too much love in you to do so. Why hate on me when I can be loving myself genuinely and consistently, receiving the positive benefits of this action.

WATCH THAT MOUTH!

Watch that mouth! Not the size or shape, not the teeth or those gums, but your flapping, pinkish-red tongue. Proverbs 18 verse 21 begins, "Death and life are in the power of the tongue:..." No truer statement concerning speech has ever been made. Throughout human history, men and women have been equally seduced and betrayed by the tongue. Nations have been built and destroyed on their words, gone to war, and made peace after broken promises, threats, or slights.

Words have the power to save, create, and destroy. Every few minutes or so, someone is murdered because of what essentially boils down to the words that came out of someone's mouth. Constantly, relationships are irreparably damaged over the wrong words being said or maybe the right words but in the wrong way.

We seem to be more comfortable using our words to break others down than building them up. We opt instead to be harbingers of hate. Why are we gossiping instead of growing up? Or constantly using our mouths to hate and not congratulate? Why aren't we guarding our thoughts better? Protect your mouth, and it will protect you. The thing is, a lot of us are sporting damaged characters and seem all right with it. In today's society, we would instead film an argument on our smartphones, hoping it will escalate rather than intervening with a kind or sensible word to diffuse the tension because sensible resolutions won't get you trending on your social media accounts as well as someone being assaulted or murdered - right?

Let's set aside all random acts of violence and every situation that gets ugly or turns deadly, and what's left has more than likely begun with a volley of destructive words. The decision for (you), a woman, to guard your words and keep your mouth shut could save your life. But on a lesser note, it can save you financially and keep Haters at bay. When

Love Thy Self

you engage in harmful, hostile, derogatory, expletive-filled exchanges, you open yourself up to the possibility of attack, which could lead to your destruction.

Your mouth can defeat you or complete you. For those of you thinking about fellatio or cunnilingus, please press pause. I'm talking about negative thought, which breeds negative words that have no substance once they cross your lips, versus positive thought, which gives birth to positive affirmation, the bedrock of a woman's spiritual foundation and the center of ourselves where we begin to love SELF. If your words are baseless, there is no basis for them, and your mouth should be closed.

If the words spewing from your mouth are malicious, demeaning, and destructive, then your mouth is nothing more than a garbage can that mirrors your heart. We are not talking about your heart with the aortas and ventricles. We're talking about the heart of your mind. The very essence of your thoughts. The place where you form the words you speak. I've been lied to, defamed, and blamed for things I sometimes knew nothing about because someone wanted attention or a free lunch. But I wouldn't be where I am today if I allowed what came out of another person's mouth to affect my movements.

Do you think you have haters? Mine are legion and know no bounds to their depravity, but if I stop to address each one, that's the attention I'm not paying to my business to turn a profit or uplift myself with positivity. Make no mistake, I am where I am in part because of my mouth. I needed to talk my way through closed doors and give high-pitched screams, shattering some glass ceilings to establish my credentials. However, because of my love for SELF, I learned quickly when and where the appropriate times to speak are. Plenty of times, I allowed my mouth to destroy plans and inhibit growth. Everything we think isn't meant to be said. If this were the case, the world would be telepathic.

{HERE ARE A FEW TIPS THAT'LL HELP RESTRAIN YOUR MOUTH}

Love Thy Self

1. Mind your business. There are 24hrs in a day/ 12 to mind your business and 12 to leave others alone
2. Before you speak, ask yourself if this is the appropriate time and place for what you have to say
3. Say what you mean in an articulate manner and mean what you say positively
4. If your intention is to bring harm with your words, keep your mouth closed

This last is very important. It is the equivalent of the genie being out of the bottle. It's damn near impossible to get it back in. Once words roll off the tongue, they can't be undone. Watch your mouth and who you are around when you speak. Your words in the wrong ears can do irreparable harm to your work, reputation and personal life. When you love yourself, you practice discretion.

WATCH YOUR MOUTH!!!

VOLUNTARY SURRENDER

{Let Love Win}

"Life's greatest battles can only be won by full surrender."

- Michelle Richard Knopf

Make no mistake: women are at war on two fronts. We are in a state of open conflict with ourselves and others concerning everything from our speech to how we dress, choose to reproduce or not reproduce, have sex, work, discipline our children, who we choose as life partners, what our bodies should or should not look like... There is a list that stretches almost into infinity. I will not ask you to cease your war with others concerning what is correct and/or beneficial for you and yours. I will ask that you stop your war with SELF. Right here and now, I'd like to see you effect a Voluntary Surrender.

Love Thy Self

Read the above quote from Michelle Richard Knopf again. Meditate on what it means. Some battles with others can be won outright if you stop warring with Self. Don't surrender to negative criticism of Self from others. Don't surrender to the unnecessary negativity you might bring from challenging your value to this world. Please don't surrender to abuse in any form. I want you to surrender to commonsense, purpose, need, and, more importantly, to Love Thy Self.

You have no control or imminent power over haters to make them stop hating, so why would you engage them, absorbing their negative energy and allowing it to detract from a positive you? The greatest battle we will ever face is with SELF. When we surrender, focusing on loving what others and sometimes even we may have deemed unlovable, we win. Voluntary Surrender is the path of least resistance, which leads to Self Love.

Women are often oppressed and misused because we enter into agreements that allow for this behavior to happen to us. Meaning we get some "good dick," financial compensation in the form of bills being paid, designer labels being given, and some "great head" and agree to be someone's bitch, hoe, or side chick. Which oftentimes turns into us relinquishing our bodies as dick depositories for men we don't really know. Before we know it, nine months later, we are officially baby moma number #3 with all of the drama that comes with the title.

Surrender to the positive attributes that are in us all. Stop fighting with them and allow them free reign over your life. The worst battle any of us women can have is with ourselves. I have learned that I can be my worst enemy or best friend. I love having myself as a friend, but friendship with myself didn't evolve overnight. I had to learn to be accepting of my positive qualities and how to make peace with myself so the battle would stop. Finally, I effected a voluntary surrender and let the love of SELF win. Why? I got tired of showing behaviors contrary to me, saying, "Hell yeah, I love me!" Knowing that it wasn't true, I started loving me in actionable terms and not empty verbal terms.

Love Thy Self

Why do we self-harm? I'm not talking about cutting or burning ourselves, but doing shit that we know or are at least 75% percent sure could end up harmful for us. I did detrimental things because I didn't care what happened to me at the time. Then, the more I watched my children's growth, the more I began to care about being present for them. I knew I needed to show more love for SELF so they would receive greater love from me.

Have you ever battled with yourself in a Cold War sort of way? I mean, doing all the dirty, underhanded shit you can to impede your evolution to womanhood, except beating your own ass or shooting yourself. Some of us will take things further and maneuver ourselves into a position to be abused by others or create situations for them to harm us. Is your lack of love for SELF so great that you're one of these women? If so, read the following aloud with the rest of us while looking in the mirror;

** I GIVE UP AND GIVE IN TO LOVING THY SELF. I NO LONGER WANT TO LOSE AT LIFE WHILE

Debra A. Antney

WAGING AN UNWINNABLE WAR BATTLING ME, MYSELF & IS A STRAIN ON MY LIFE THAT I CAN NO LONGER AFFORD. I AM READY TO LET LOVE WIN. CONSIDER THIS MY VOLUNTARY SURRENDER **

MORE "LIKES THAN LOVE

Who's creeping in your DM? How do you feel about the comments coming in about what you just posted? Are you really at your best with one hundred forty characters or less? Will Tick Tock get you off the block? What type of photos can you snap, or how much gossip can you chat? What else can you do to increase your Facebook profile to upgrade your lifestyle? I wonder!

When I was growing up, there was no social media. Social media for me was a group of us congregating on my parent's porch or a friend's stoop back in Queens. We talked our shit on Ma Bell (landline phone) or face to face, not behind screens of bits & bytes. I (lmao) laughed my ass off when I first heard about a Twitter fight. What kind of fight is this? The earrings and heels don't even have to come off, and the wigs and hair extensions are safe.

Don't mistake me; the internet and its bastardized child "social media" are two of the greatest inventions since the wheel and the cellphone. It allows new relationships to be formed, information, and ideas to be exchanged. This excellent medium allows someone to reach out using keystrokes who otherwise might know they existed. I use it to communicate with hundreds of thousands of women just like you. It is definitely an essential tool in today's society.

The real problem for me is how women betray themselves by poorly portraying themselves. The lewd & suggestive photographs posted without receiving compensation. The disrespectful and derogatory comments are thrown around to create sensationalism to generate more "likes." The internet was designed as an information resource and computerized super highway to bring the world closer together. We're supposed to be learning while establishing friends. Instead, many of us are becoming real-world enemies.

Love Thy Self

Face to face as a kid, if we did something terrible or offensive, we apologized, "I take it back" and kept it moving. Now, as adults on the internet using social media, we don't have that luxury. This bastard is ornery as fuck! The internet won't let us take anything back. Before we can sweep it or delete it, someone has taken a screengrab to parade it over every site for the world to see. When we hate on others or say and do stupid shit on social media, it is virtually there forever. It doesn't matter that your conscience got the better of you, and there was a change of heart. "I'll take it down!" Too late!

The pursuit of "likes" has overshadowed love, especially love for SELF. In the future, when you log in, be sure to show the respect you want to be granted. Don't set aside love for "likes." Increase your profile through positive postings. Social media has simple rules of etiquette: Can my parents, preacher, priest, or employer read or view what I've posted? Answer this question honestly and save a lot of trouble.

THIRSTY BY NATURE??

{O.P.P.}

Before I get into this subject matter, I want those with sensitive ears and fragile emotional states to skip ahead. The following is for grown-ass women with mature, open minds. Okay, here we go;

What I am about to impart to you women is more for edification than empowerment & motivation. However, some of you will receive those things, too, after reading this material. You may be empowered to free your mind or be motivated to change it altogether. The thing is, you'll only know once you reach that destination in your thoughts.

The subject I want to address is THIRSTINESS. How many of us are THIRSTY BY NATURE?? Let me explain in detail so that you can come to a clear understanding. Lately, I've been running into two kinds of women. The Young & Restless and The

Mature & Thankless. The younger women I've been in contact with have the Mojave desert running through the crack of their asses. Meaning they are thirsty for sex and companionship, either for all of the wrong reasons or reasons that are born from misguided thoughts. They're begging for liquid as long as it's financial. The mature women are no better, acting like fish. They claim to be wet and willing, though they can't get hooked up to save their lives. Why?

Let's start with the Young & Restless. There are a few different categories of these women. The first is:

Ms. Iwanna Bag - This is the young woman who "wants" but isn't willing to work for what she wants, so she uses her pussy and steps over and on her "friends" as a shortcut. We who are wiser and more mature know that shortcuts of this kind are similar to those in a horror film. A woman separates from her family and genuine friends, becomes lost, and will more than likely get hurt by someone or something unexpected.

So & So's Bitch - No one cares what her actual name is because she is really only identified by or through her partner. Why? It's enough for her that her significant other has lucrative finances, is considered "somebody" important, and she can leech off of their substantial means and identity instead of creating one of her own.

Meme` Tentwo - She is young and restless for sure. Patience doesn't reside in her being; she is all about instant gratification. She wants it NOW and is willing to sexually outperform an Atlanta stripper and a Red light district whore combined to get it. Her actions are constantly screaming selfishly, "ME, ME! And like hands on a broken clock, her legs are locked in the ten & two positions for those willing to provide for her needs and desires. She keeps claiming to love herself, but her actions are so loud that it's hard to hear or see any truth in her proclamations.

These women are a danger to themselves and those in their circles. They reek of desperation, need, and want, and yet, they don't even know

Love Thy Self

what their true needs or wants are. Don't be one of these young women, and if you think you are, CHANGE.

The Mature & Thankless are a little different. These women, for the most part, have come up already. To anyone peering through the glass walls of their life, they seem as if their shit is together. They are riding well, living well, and looking even better. But these women live in an ocean teeming with life and are thirsty.

They tell me, "Ms. Deb, I'm a little older, but my pussy stay wet. I need a man! I enjoy sex, but these men are tripping!" Some of these beautiful women only stay wet because they don't know the difference between vaginal moisture due to arousal and feminine urinary incontinence due to an overactive bladder. I'm going to solve half of their problems right now... Isle 69, Poise pads, or depends.

To the rest of these mature women, I ask, "Why do you need a man or partner of any kind to complete what is already whole?" If you aren't whole, you should love SELF to get whole. A "man/partner" should be like paint on a wall, expensive rims on a vehicle, jewelry on a woman's person, or clothes covering her body. Hell, even a good wig . . . Accentuating what is already there to make it better or appear better. Why aren't these incredible women more thankful for who they are? This is something only they can answer.

Some of my mature sisters (women) are chasing dicks or other sexual conquests as if it owes them back child support. Stop it! Do you hear me? Just stop it! A woman can only get ahead in a relationship for so long by giving head. This type of behavior smacks of desperation. Truthfully, the Mature & Thankless are fucking more than The Young & Restless. The only thing separating them is discretion and financial desire. The mature woman usually has her own.

There is no other person on this planet who should know your pussy better than you. Seeking satisfaction from outside sources can leave a woman thirsty when that source dries up or is cut off. Maturity is supposed to bring about wisdom. Maybe these mature, thankless women can't find suitable relations because they are unwise in their pursuits?

ARE YOU DOWN WITH O.P.P.?
If not, you better get down with it!

Operating your own
Pussy to achieve
Pleasure without being disrespected!

This anecdote is for The Young & Restless, and The Mature & Thankless. I'm going to make some dicks and a few pussies upset with what I will drop on you, readers. I'm introducing you to an effective tool to combat sexual thirstiness, I'm giving you some real advice on The Young & Restless, who self-exploit for profit. Here's that tool . . . MASTURBATION!! That's right, join the masturbation nation.

I will tell you why masturbation is an effective tool against thirstiness and dick desperation. No

Love Thy Self

partner on the planet can rock your world better than you can, girl!!

WHOSE IS IT?

It better be yours! I wish a motherfucker would ask me, "WHOSE PUSSY IS THIS?" It definitely isn't yours, MAN. If any of us is dumb enough to give ownership of our high commodity vagina to someone, then we deserve whatever comes our way in terms of disappointment and deceit. If he's supplying it with multiple orgasms regularly and his ass is willing to pay for monthly Vagisil general maintenance, plus walk around with it for five to seven days out of that same month while its bleeding and cramping, or take on menopause with its hot & cold flashes . . . ? Fuck it! I'm willing to work out a short-term lease agreement for that type of dedication.

We more mature women know this person is a rarity. So, let's keep it pushing. "WHOSE PUSS8Y IS IT?" Oh, it's most certainly mine, And just as I am responsible for its cleaning, care & comfort, I am also responsible for its coming to orgasm. Whether

Love Thy Self

I choose to manually manipulate my vagina with the digital dexterity of a classical pianist or shoot pleasure into my clitoris with a bullet that I own, operate, and can pull the trigger on at will, is my business, and Ms. Deb takes her business seriously!

How can a woman indeed be satisfied unless she's thoroughly self-explored the parameters of what pleases her? We can choose phallus size, how we work the stroke and tempo to reach a climactic crescendo, getting shit right every time. Why don't we? I don't need a partner to satisfy me nor should any woman read this.

Herein lies the real problem. The [thought] of need of a partner, [is a senseless one]. NEED implies that you can't do without. Follow my belief on this matter... If you need a partner, you are susceptible to being beguiled, beaten, financially swindled, and generally fucked over. Not just once but like the orgasms you seek multiple times. The need is a condition or situation which must be met or supplied in order for you to maintain. Now, apply this definition to a woman thinking she needs a partner.

Does this mean a woman ain't shit without someone to validate or authenticate who she is? In some of our minds, YES!! We all know a woman who is a magnet for troubled relationships. Why? Her NEED increases her susceptibility to bullshit & abuse because it pressures her to settle. That misconception is entrenched in her brain, which tells her, "You NEED someone! You can't be by yourself! Don't you like having someone to talk to? Don't you like sex?" Is wrong. Let me break this down.... You can be by yourself when you LOVE SELF. Do you need someone to talk with? Google Dionne Warwick -THAT'S WHAT FRIENDS ARE FOR! As for sex?

With attention to detail and practice, no partner will ever know your pussy better than you. IT'S YOURS!! Own it. Be responsible for your own pleasure.

Masturbation eradicates the NEED for a partner while increasing your desire for the best potential partner. Let's imagine going on a date with someone whom you consider attractive and exciting. At the time of your date, you are six months without sex. Right before your date, masturbate vigorously until you reach at least two orgasms. I bet after your date, that person isn't as interesting or attractive. Fucking yourself can prevent you from being fucked over. For those of us with "DICK DESPERATION," - This is, "I need a dick to feel like a natural woman." You are only exposing yourself as a hearty hoe.

In all seriousness, masturbation is one of the keys to not only a healthy sex life but an inhibitor of a woman being deceived by "dick desperation". It will help you learn the principles of your pleasure so that you are able to instruct the right partner on how to satisfy you continuously. In addition, masturbation breeds a strong sense of self-confidence. It helps fortify a woman's belief that she can (O)perate her own (P)ussy to achieve (P)leisure without allowing anyone to disrespect her, or I should add, allowing her thirsty self to be opened up to disrespect.

The Mature & Thankless are notorious for eschewing the benefits of masturbation. I've heard it all... "Deb, why would I do that with all this good dick out here?"... "I just got my vampire nails done, I ain't trying to hurt myself."... "My fingers can't suck it the way that mouth does."... Then, on the flip side, I've heard... "I treated my partner so good! Why did they do me like this, Deb?"... "He fucked me into a coma and the next thing I know, my money's gone, credit screwed up; why didn't I see it coming?"... "We done made up. He slapped me because I got loud with him, but last night was so special. I came so much, I didn't know where I was going. I love him!"

Dick can be a dis-ease that makes you go deaf, dumb, and blind if you are thirsty for it. It's pretty much like not eating for a couple of days and having a meal. Even though that food is subpar, you're wolfing it down like it's the last supper because you are hungry. Masturbation fills that hunger so your palate can discern bullshit from spaghetti Bolognese. A great many of us are wolfing down a dick with a side of "fucked over" and grinning like Cheshire cats who just caught the canary. Make it make some damn sense!

Masturbation is a healthy form of self-love that creates a strong shield of self-confidence that protects you from a lot of stress and strife in your sex life that can spill over into other areas of your being. Be smart and learn to make love to yourself in hopes that you'll be able to recognize when it is shown to you by others.

Now for The Young & Restless; Why are you so reckless? When I was growing up, there was a slick-talking pimp on every corner attempting to use his voice box to make a P.Y.T. (Pretty Young Thing) sell her tight box to make some money. Now, every P.Y.T. is exploiting herself for a paycheck, which pales in comparison to her priceless-ness. WHY?

Let me preface the following by stating clearly that I am not talking about women getting paid for their legitimate jobs, i.e. Instagram models, Adult industry stars, strippers, and honest-to-goodness Hoes (prostitutes). I am referring to those of you who are gold-digging, sack-chasing, side chicks for Cash/Dash. Cash is monetary currency, and Dash is designer gear in lieu of cash. I'm calling out The Young & Restless along with a few of you who are old enough to be their mothers but are still slanging your head and ass for Cash/Dash with no end in sight.

You women know exactly who you are. You're the ones who plot, plan, and strategize how to proffer your pussy for pay for daily survival with complete disregard for what harm you might bring to SELF and others along the way. You are classified as someone's, Bitch, Hoe, Side Chick, or Trick, and really don't care because the magic is in the Cash/Dash. Sadly, you don't plot for your come-up, won't plan for your future, or systematically strategize for your long-term survival.

Women . . . Regardless of size, age, race, financial background or political leaning, rule the world!

Love Thy Self

Why would you exploit yourself for what amounts to peanuts when you're worth a million times more than diamonds at the very least? If you feel self-exploitation is a must, then do so with a plan to come up and stay up! But treating your vagina like an ATM requires a mindset that is detrimental in the short & long term if left unchecked.

I know women who are proud to receive monetary compensation for performing sex acts. I know one in particular who drives an expensive foreign car, wears the finest in designer apparel and lives like a rapper. She's a beautiful, tortured soul who has sold her peace of mind for a piece of a lifestyle she could acquire through other means, rather than engaging in side chick sex for some blue strips (hundred dollar bills) or a designer bag. For sure, she is capable of running her own business and being a CEO. Instead she's content with living off what her sexual partners provide in the form of payments or gifts for the use of her three main holes.

Listen closely, ladies . . . I firmly believe that everyone born of the female gender starts life with a three million dollar trust fund and an unlimited credit supply. Oral, vaginal, anal / mouth, pussy, ass! The three main holes. Attribute a million-dollar tag to each and imagine it being stored in a trust that you can access in dire emergencies.

For instance, There's no other way to pay your rent, and the landlord is evicting you and your children. You reach into that trust, suck some dick and keep a roof over your children's heads. I ain't judging! But for those of us sucking that same dick to get a designer bag . . . I'm telling you that your mind is an unlimited supply of credit. It will allow you to get what you desire from your thoughts & ideas. Use your intellect, sheer determination, and womanly willpower and own the store that the bag is sold out of. I keep mentioning the "BAG" because you'll keep saying it. "I need the bag!" . . . "I'm in my bag!" . . . "I gotta get a bag!" . . . "My bag ain't big enough!" Why are you concerned about a "BAG"

Love Thy Self

more than your life? Self-exploitation is never a good thing. Loving Your SELF is!!

STRESS

Right now, I'm feeling pretty good, but there are times when I'm a mess because I'm stressed.

Usually, it happens when business matters are piling up on me, or I'm trying to get my house in order. Then there are those other times when my family, friends, or significant other of the moment just get on my damn nerves with everything from A to Z. I'm screaming inside the confines of my mind, "Lord, please help me before I fuck one of them up!" At these chaotic times, I have to step back and breathe. Really! I mean, actually stopping what I'm doing, centering myself and taking a few deep, calming breaths, forcing myself to be cool. If I don't, then I might do something irrational, like be brutally honest, which often leads to more conflict. [SIDE NOTE: There is a time for brutal honesty with others, and that time should usually be premeditated.] Anyway . . . Who needs more drama? I certainly don't.

Love Thy Self

What's STRESS? It is the mental worry, pressure, or frustration. It's force causing strain.

Where does it come from? You! Stress begins and ends with SELF.

How can it be prevented or excised from your life? Positive thought.

Is it dangerous? Very much so.

How does it affect the people around you? . . . . .

STRESS is mental worry which lends itself to frustration and a person feeling under pressure. It comes from all situations, though it can't survive without you as its host. Stress only has a home if you invite it in. It is negative in origin. It's like a germ or parasite that needs the proper environment to exist. If you allow someone, someplace or something to exert overwhelming force upon your mental, emotional, or spiritual state until it causes strain, altering who you genuinely are, then, of course, you will feel it.

Debra A. Antney

At my age, with the accumulated life experience I have at my disposal, I should know better than to allow myself to be stressed out. But there have been times when I've become upset, throwing good sense and caution to the curb while keeping the garbage with me. How foolish is that? It takes either a great effort to remain positive in the face of adversity or continued practice until it becomes a natural response. What kind of {practice}? The practice of patience, tolerance, and peace. You'll become stronger each time you face stress and apply these three attributes. Not physically, but emotionally, mentally, and spiritually, and this strength will carry you through any stressful situation.

A woman must be strong to deal with stress. Though most of us don't practice the strength training necessary for those positive parts of us to do the heavy lifting when stress rears its ugly head. You know, things like . . . not worrying, exercising patience, showing love for self, being tolerable of those who seem intolerable, and foregoing negativity.

This bitch STRESS is a rapacious hunter of the weak-minded, easily misled and the hateful. If you accept it, your hair will fall out. You will become lethargic, lose weight, gain weight, get sick . . . And my all-time favorite: DEPRESSION! This jackass will move in on you like termites and eat away at your joy. It will throw a dark, obscure cloud over your entire life. Without self-help, professional therapy, and love for yourself, you won't see through the misery, and others won't be able to see you. They will only see your problems, and you'll be ostracized and mislabeled.

Stress can have you contemplating suicide or on the verge of committing a homicide, depending on its severity. Yes, it is just that dangerous. Your stress affects the people within your sphere of influence {circle}. The strain you're under can affect the husband, wife, life partner, family, friends, co-workers, or employees. A woman's mood and how she communicates or doesn't with the people in her life can create adverse situations that can irreparably damage these relationships.

HERE ARE FIVE THINGS TO DO WHEN STRESSED:

1) Take an adult timeout. Find a quiet place to rest your mind and gather your thoughts.
2) Engage in a positive activity.
3) Immediately address the source of the strain. End it before it can end you.
4) Play your favorite music, letting it soothe your soul, then reset.
5) Have SEX! Wait... Let me clarify - Good SEX! Bad sex will only add insult to injury.

Sometimes, it's good to just talk about what's stressing you out. There is nothing wrong with speaking with a mental health professional. The stigma attached to speaking to a therapist, behavioral psychologist, or psychiatrist is wrong. If things aren't severe, try talking to a friend or family member. If you feel uncomfortable doing that because you're worried about your business ending up as gossip, go to the mirror and talk it out with the woman you see there. If she tells someone your business, then you really do have issues. Each woman is responsible for allowing STRESS into her life. If you don't want it, DON'T ACCEPT IT!

There is an ancient Twi proverb that says;

"You must eat the elephant one bite at a time."

This means that to deal with any problem we must be thoughtful, patient, rational, positive, caring, loving and first, kind to ourselves, then others. One bite at a time the elephant is to be chewed on until it's gone. In the proverb, the elephant is the problem. In reality, it's YOU! You need to be chewed on one bite at a time or, rather, worked on step by step, priceless piece by priceless piece, until the necessary corrections for improvement have been made. To better yourself is to better the world. Stay blessed and not stressed.

These eleven short topics are enough to prompt any woman to start thinking about her present and future self. I only want for you what you should want for yourself... GROWTH! If you must destroy the current female that you are in order to become the woman you need and wish to be to attain the heights of success you aspire to, start by eradicating all things negative from your life, then build upward from there.

To ascertain the height of success you envision requires you to get deep with SELF. This starts with being extremely forthright and honest with the woman in the mirror. More importantly, I think it worthy to note; NO RECONSTRUCTION OF SELF CAN SUCCESSFULLY TAKE PLACE WITHOUT THE DEMOLITION OF "OLD SELF". Those nasty, bad habits which are no good for growth must be destroyed.

Once an honest inventory is taken of all the (negative) bad broken shit that you think is detrimental to a successful lifestyle and is thrown out and/or fixed, you can effectively plan a positive prosperous future for SELF.

Love Thy Self

** This last topic is near and dear to my heart. Let's do a quick recap before we get to it: . . .

1. WE'RE ALL AVERAGE (Until We're Not)
2. WHAT IS LOVE?
3. P.U.S.S.Y. IS POWER
4. SETTLING
5. WHY HATE ON ME?
6. WATCH THAT MOUTH!
7. VOLUNTARY SURRENDER
8. MORE "LIKES" THAN LOVE
9. THIRSTY BY NATURE (O.P.P.)
10. WHOSE IS IT?
11. STRESS

. . . All of these lead to the following topic, which is the first rule of nature. If loving thy neighbor is considered the Golden Rule, then to love thyself is most definitely platinum. SELF PRESERVATION is our twelfth topic. It is integral to everything you've read within this guide.

SELF PRESERVATION

Some of us women don't care about self-preservation because we mistakenly believe we have nothing about ourselves worth preserving. Why do some of us find it difficult to protect ourselves and one another from destruction and harm? We should all want to remain alive for as long as humanly possible and live as well as we can while doing so. Protection from harm or misfortune is inherently vital to our health. I'm speaking about mental, emotional, sexual, and financial health.

Through lack of exercising the sheer will to avoid pain and destruction to SELF, we women must understand that we are often our first abusers by and through our acceptance of bad acts and underperformance. This simply means we are doing or accepting things contradictory to positive living. We must guard against this type of destructive behavior from us or others.

Debra A. Antney

If we aren't looking out for number #1, trust that we'll be swimming up the creek in a lot of number #2. Now, don't get all self-absorbed on me and use the above line about looking out for number one as an excuse to act petty and selfish. I'm simply imploring women to use commonsense, logic, intelligence and deductive reasoning to determine positive solutions for all of your problems while keeping your best interest uppermost in mind.

Self-preservation should be paramount in the lives of all women, especially if she has children or is a guardian. We women are considered the "root" from which all children grow (humanity). We must preserve ourselves in hopes that the future will grow and flourish. Make no mistake: women are the essential backbone of every community, whether it's a village in Botswana or a neighborhood in Baltimore. Show me well-rounded, mature, strong women, and I'll show you a thriving society with women at the forefront. We are what makes the world turn. There is no better time to be of our gender than heading into the

Love Thy Self

second quarter of the twenty-first century. Yes, there is still discrimination, thick glass ceilings, and those who don't want to see us rise. Still, we have been afforded the tools to deal decidedly with one while shattering the other.

****

UNTIL NEXT TIME

"Right here, I am going to press pause. I truly want you women to think heavily about this MINI M.E.G. while making some serious and, for some, much-needed changes that will benefit you and yours. Don't panic; this motivational empowerment guide, "LOVE THY SELF" is just the beginning of a dedicated series. Until next time, I'm Debra Antney, celebrity manager, television and music producer, Reality television star, author, daughter, sister, mother, grandmother, Atlanta's aunt, lover . . . Though most importantly, lover of SELF. Cool beans!

www.ingramcontent.com/pod-product-compliance
Lightning Source LLC
LaVergne TN
LVHW061040070526
838201LV00073B/5129